Reading for TODAY

Introductory Book

D1608680

Program Authors

**Linda Ward Beech • James W. Beers • Jo Ann Dauzat
Sam V. Dauzat • Tara McCarthy**

Program Consultants

Myra K. Baum
Office of Adult and
    Continuing Education
Brooklyn, New York

Francis J. Feltman, Jr.
Racine Youth Offender
    Correctional Facility
Racine, Wisconsin

Mary Ann Guilliams
Gary Job Corps
San Marcos, Texas

Julie Jacobs
Inmate Literacy Project
Santa Clara County Library
Milpitas, California

Maxine L. McCormick
Workforce Education
Orange County Public Schools
Orlando, Florida

Sandra S. Owens
Laurens County Literacy Council
Laurens, South Carolina

STECK-VAUGHN
ELEMENTARY · SECONDARY · ADULT · LIBRARY

A Harcourt Company

www.steck-vaughn.com

Acknowledgments

Staff Credits

Executive Editor: Ellen Northcutt
Senior Editor: Donna Townsend
Associate Design Director: Joyce Spicer
Supervising Designer: Pamela Heaney
Designer: Jessica Bristow
Production Coordinator: Rebecca Gonzales
Electronic Production Artists: Julia Miracle-Hagaman and Karen Wilburn
Senior Technical Advisor: Alan Klemp
Electronic Production Specialist: Dina Bahan

Photography Credits

Photography by Park Street Photography; Digital Studios, Austin, Texas; Artville; Corbis; Eyewire; iSwoop; PhotoDisc.

Additional photography by: Cover (engine) ©Berle Cherney/Uniphoto; p.11 (money) ©John Neubauer/PhotoEdit; p.12 (people) ©SuperStock; p.15 (sick) ©Alan Thomton/Stone; p.26 (money) ©John Neubauer/PhotoEdit; p.27 (dam) ©David Ball/The Stock Market; p.29 (gate) ©Robert W. Ginn/Unicorn Stock Photos; p.29 (game) ©John Lei/Stock Boston; p.30 (dam) ©David Ball/The Stock Market; p.33 (game) ©John Lei/Stock Boston; p.33 (money) ©John Neubauer/PhotoEdit; p.34 (dam) ©David Ball/The Stock Market; p.38 (sick) ©Alan Thomton/Stone; p.38 (seed) ©Maximilian Stock LTD/Earth Scenes; p.38 (gate) ©Robert W. Ginn/Unicorn Stock Photos; p.41 (otter) ©Mark Newman/Bruce Coleman, Inc.; p.41 (sick) ©Alan Thomton/Stone; p.41 (ostrich) ©Laura Riley/Bruce Coleman, Inc.; pp.41, 43, 44 (ox) ©Russell Grunake/Unicorn Stock Photos; p.44 (dam) ©David Ball/The Stock Market; p.48 (judge) ©Dennis MacDonald/Unicorn Stock Photos; p.49 (people) ©SuperStock; p.52 (igloo) ©David Roseberg/Stone; p.52 (insulation) ©Alvin Henry/The Stock Market; p.52 (ox) ©Russell Grunake/Unicorn Stock Photos; p.53 (dam) ©David Ball/The Stock Market; pp.54, 55 (sick) ©Alan Thomton/Stone; p.58 (otter) ©Mark Newman/Bruce Coleman, Inc.; p.59 (hive) ©Ken Stepnell/Bruce Coleman, Inc.; pp.59, 63 (hug) ©Jose Pelaez Photography/The Stock Market; p.68 (volcano) ©SuperStock; p.70 (zoo) ©E. R. Degginger/Bruce Coleman, Inc.; p.70 (volcano) ©SuperStock; p.73 (hive) ©Ken Stepnell/Bruce Coleman, Inc.; p.74 (engine) ©Berle Cherney/Uniphoto; p.74 (igloo) ©David Roseberg/Stone; p.76 (zoo) ©E. R. Degginger/Bruce Coleman, Inc.; p.76 (volcano) ©SuperStock; p.77 (hive) ©Ken Stepnell/Bruce Coleman, Inc.; p.80 (dam) ©David Ball/The Stock Market; p.81 (zoo) ©E. R. Degginger/Bruce Coleman, Inc.; p.82 (gate) ©Robert W. Ginn/Unicorn Stock Photos; p.82 (game) ©John Lei/Stock Boston; p.83 (fin) ©Gerard Lacz/Peter Arnold, Inc.; p.83 (vane) ©Charles D. Winters/Photo Researchers, Inc.; p.85 (dam) ©David Ball/The Stock Market; p.85 (fin) ©Gerard Lacz/Peter Arnold, Inc.; p.86 (hive) ©Ken Stepnell/Bruce Coleman, Inc.; p.86 (gate) ©Robert W. Ginn/Unicorn Stock Photos; p.91 (flute) ©Park Street; p.92 (hug) ©Jose Pelaez Photography/The Stock Market; p.93 (flute) ©Park Street; p.96 (seal) ©Fred Bruemmer/Peter Arnold, Inc.; p.96 (teeth) ©SuperStock; p.96 (weed) ©Gabe Palmer/The Stock Market; p.96 (tree) ©West, Ian Osf/Earth Scenes; p.97 (bee) ©Stephen Dalton/Animals Animals; p.97 (team) ©Robert E. Daemmrich/Stone; p.98 (tree) ©West, Ian Osf/Earth Scenes; p.98 (bee) ©Stephen Dalton/Animals Animals; p.98 (seal) ©Fred Bruemmer/Peter Arnold, Inc.; p.98 (weed) ©Gabe Palmer/The Stock Market; p.103 (weed) ©Gabe Palmer/The Stock Market; p.105 (hug) ©Jose Pelaez Photography/The Stock Market; p.105 (vane) ©Charles D. Winters/Photo Researchers, Inc.; p.105 (gate) ©Robert W. Ginn/Unicorn Stock Photos; p.106 (dam) ©David Ball/The Stock Market; p.106 (zoo) ©E. R. Degginger/Bruce Coleman, Inc.; p.107 (hive) ©Ken Stepnell/Bruce Coleman, Inc.; p.107 (fin) ©Gerard Lacz/Peter Arnold, Inc.

ISBN 07398-2838-X

Contents

To the Learner

In this book you will learn the name of each letter in the alphabet. The alphabet has 26 letters. You will also learn the sounds the letters stand for. You will write the letters in small and capital letters. Learning the letters is the first step in learning to read. Learning the sounds is the second step.

Reading words is the next step. Learning any skill takes a lot of practice. Reading is a skill that you must practice. As you learn new words, please write the words in a notebook or journal as well as using these pages. This book gives you the practice to become good at the skill of reading. Have a good time using this book. It is written for you!

Instructor's Notes: Read this page to students. Discuss having students keep a notebook or journal of words and original sentences they write. Refer to the *Reading for Today Instructor's Guide* for the answer key and lesson plans and a discussion of how to use the Learner Placement Form on the inside back cover of this book.

Unit 1 Letters of the Alphabet

Reading Signs

Signs all around us use the alphabet.
Which signs do you know?

1.

2.

3.

4.

5.

6.

7.

8.

9.

10.

11.

12.

Instructor's Notes: Have students read the signs they recognize. Discuss the meaning of the signs. Point out that different letter styles can be used for the same word. Explain that the skills students will study in *Reading for Today* will help them read signs regardless of the letter style used.

Reading Signs

1.
Out of Order

2.
OUT OF ORDER

3.

DO NOT ENTER

4.
DO NOT ENTER

5.
Men

6.

MEN

7.

DANGER

8.
Danger!

9.
FOR SALE

10.

FOR SALE

11.

Women

12.

women

Instructor's Notes: Have students read the signs they recognize. Discuss the meaning of the signs. Point out that different letter styles can be used for the same word. Explain that the skills students will study in *Reading for Today* will help them read signs regardless of the letter style used.

Aa
apple

Bb
bed

1. Write the letters.

A a

B b

2. Circle **A** and **a**.

A O A C A F R A P F A

a o c g c a e a p c a a

at   can   ran   Ann   Al   and   an

3. Circle **B** and **b**.

B A B P B D R B A R B

b g b a b p o b c p g b

bat   cab   Bob   big   Bess   web

Instructor's Notes: Introduce the letters *Aa* and *Bb*. Say the letter names. Identify the key pictures. Tell students *apple* begins with *a* and *bed* begins with *b*. Point out the difference between the capital (upper-case) and small (lower-case) letters. Then read the directions and have students complete the activities.

3

Unit 1

Cc  car **Dd**  dog

1. **Write the letters.**

C c

D d

2. **Circle C and c.**

C O G C C D B G C O

c o c a c e o c a e c

cat cab bacon Cass Cal

3. **Circle D and d.**

D B C D G P B D D P

d a d d c b p b d p b

dog bad Dad red and Dot

Instructor's Notes: Introduce the letters *Cc* and *Dd*. Say the letter names. Identify the key pictures. Tell students *car* begins with *c* and *dog* begins with *d*. Point out the difference between the capital (upper-case) and small (lower-case) letters. Then read the directions and have students complete the activities.

4

Ee

egg

Ff

food

1. **Write the letters.**

Ee

Ff

2. **Circle E and e.**

E A E P E F T E F T

c e o e e c a e o c e

Ella bed get egg Ed red

3. **Circle F and f.**

F B F P F F E T F E

f h f b f t f f t b h f

fan Fran if fun Jeff Fred

Instructor's Notes: Introduce the letters *Ee* and *Ff*. Say the letter names. Identify the key pictures. Tell students *egg* begins with *e* and *food* begins with *f*. Point out the difference between the capital (upper-case) and small (lower-case) letters. Then read the directions and have students complete the activities.

Review Aa, Bb, Cc, Dd, Ee, Ff

1. Trace the letters.

A a B b C c D d E e F f

2. Write the letters.

3. Write the missing letters.

A B C   E

     b   d   f

4. Draw lines to match the letters.

A   b   D   f

B   c   E   d

C   a   F   e

5. Circle the letters.

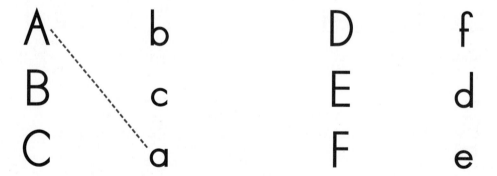

Bb | (B)ob bat box lab cab

Cc | cut cap cat cub back

Instructor's Notes: Review *Aa–Ff* together. Have students make flash cards for these letters. Read the directions. Then help as needed. For students who need extra practice in the alphabet and visual discrimination of letter shapes use Blackline Master 2, and for those needing extra practice in forming letters, use Blackline Master 1 in the *Reading for Today Instructor's Guide.*

Gg

go

Hh

home

1. Write the letters.

G g

H h

2. Circle **G** and **g**.

G C G C D G O C G

g q g c g p q g j p g

Gus egg got Peg dog gas

3. Circle **H** and **h**.

H E H E T H F H T H

h b h d p h d h f h d

Hal hill had fish he Helen

Instructor's Notes: Introduce the letters *Gg* and *Hh*. Say the letter names. Identify the key pictures. Tell students *go* begins with *g* and *home* begins with *h*. Point out the difference between the capital (upper-case) and small (lower-case) letters. Then read the directions and have students complete the activities.

I i

inch

J j

jeep

1. Write the letters.

I i

J j

2. Circle I and i.

I E I T I L T I L I E I

i i i j h i l j i l l i j i l i

in Inez quit if did is kite

3. Circle J and j.

J I J J F T G P J C J J

j i j j j g i t f g p i j f

Jan jog jam job jet Jim

Instructor's Notes: Introduce the letters *Ii* and *Jj*. Say the letter names. Identify the key pictures. Tell students *inch* begins with *i* and *jeep* begins with *j*. Point out the difference between the capital (upper-case) and small (lower-case) letters. Then read the directions and have students complete the activities.

Kk  key   Ll  light

1. Write the letters.

K k

L l

2. Circle **K** and **k**.

K T I K K R E F R B K

k l k k l t f b k d b k f

Ken kid kit sick Kim kick

3. Circle **L** and **l**.

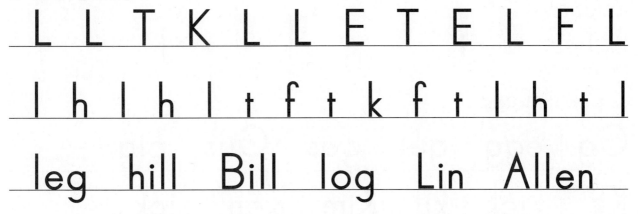

L L T K L L L E T E L F L

l h l h l t f t k f t l h t l

leg hill Bill log Lin Allen

Instructor's Notes: Introduce the letters *Kk* and *Ll*. Say the letter names. Identify the key pictures. Tell students *key* begins with *k* and *light* begins with *l*. Point out the difference between the capital (upper-case) and small (lower-case) letters. Then read the directions and have students complete the activities.

9

Unit 1

Review Gg, Hh, Ii, Jj, Kk, Ll

1. Trace the letters.

Gg Hh Ii Jj Kk Ll

2. Write the letters.

3. Write the missing letters.

H   J   L

g   i   l

4. Draw lines to match the letters.

G   i   J   k

H   h   K   l

I   g   L   j

5. Circle the letters.

Gg | egg get gas Gus pig

Kk | kick kit Kim Ken sick

Instructor's Notes: Review *Gg–Ll* together. Have students make flash cards for these letters. Read the directions. Then help as needed. For students who need extra practice in the alphabet and visual discrimination of letter shapes use Blackline Master 2, and for those needing extra practice in forming letters, use Blackline Master 1 in the *Reading for Today Instructor's Guide.*

Mm

money

Nn

nurse

1. Write the letters.

M m

N n

2. Circle **M** and **m**.

M   N   M   W   M   V   W   M   N

u   n   u   m   m   n   n   u   m   n   w   w

man   met   Mom   ham   Tom   miss

3. Circle **N** and **n**.

N   N   M   N   N   V   M   N   V   M

n   u   n   u   n   m   v   n   n   m   v   n   u

not   Ned   nut   Nan   net   fun

Instructor's Notes: Introduce the letters *Mm* and *Nn*. Say the letter names. Identify the key pictures. Tell students *money* begins with *m* and *nurse* begins with *n*. Point out the difference between the capital (upper-case) and small (lower-case) letters. Read the directions and have students complete the activities.

O o

olive

P p

people

1. Write the letters.

O o

P p

2. Circle O and o.

O Q O O C D Q O C

o c o o o a c o a c o

off on Mom not log pot

3. Circle P and p.

P B P B P P F B R P

p q p d p b q p p b d

pan Pam cup pop Pat pen

Instructor's Notes: Introduce the letters *Oo* and *Pp*. Say the letter names. Identify the key pictures. Tell students *olive* begins with *o* and *people* begins with *p*. Point out the difference between the capital (upper-case) and small (lower-case) letters. Read the directions and have students complete the activities.

Qq

quarter

Rr

radio

1. Write the letters.

Q q

R r

2. Circle Q and q.

Q O Q Q C C O Q O

g q q p q p q q g p g

quiet quit quiz Quinn quilt

3. Circle R and r.

R P R D R P F R B R

r r n r u f r r n f p r

Rob ran red rug car Ron

Instructor's Notes: Introduce the letters *Qq* and *Rr*. Say the letter names. Identify the key pictures. Tell students *quarter* begins with *q.* and *radio* begins with *r.* Point out the difference between the capital (upper-case) and small (lower-case) letters. Then read the directions and have students complete the activities.

Review Mm, Nn, Oo, Pp, Qq, Rr

1. Trace the letters.

Mm Nn Oo Pp Qq Rr

2. Write the letters.

3. Write the missing letters.

M   P   R

o   q

4. Draw lines to match the letters.

M   m   P   q

N   o   Q   p

O   n   R   r

5. Circle the letters.

Mm | man   ham   met   Matt   am

Qq | quit   liquid   quick   Quinn

Instructor's Notes: Review *Mm–Rr* together. Have students make flash cards for these letters. Read the directions. Then help as needed. For students who need extra practice in the alphabet and visual discrimination of letter shapes use Blackline Master 2, and for those needing extra practice in forming letters, use Blackline Master 1 in the *Reading for Today Instructor's Guide*.

S s

sick

T t

table

1. Write the letters.

S s

T t

2. Circle S and s.

S G S O S B S S J B

s c s s o e a s c a s e o

sun sit sat Sam gas Sara

3. Circle T and t.

T J T I T L F T E I T L

t t l i t f l t t i f l t i

top tan Tom Tess cat letter

Instructor's Notes: Introduce the letters *Ss* and *Tt*. Say the letter names. Identify the key pictures. Tell students *sick* begins with *s* and *table* begins with *t*. Point out the difference between the capital (upper-case) and small (lower-case) letters. Then read the directions and have students complete the activities.

15

Unit 1

Uu

umbrella

Vv

van

1. Write the letters.

U u

V v

2. Circle **U** and **u**.

U C U O U U V N U

u n u u m v e v u n u

us gum bus up rub cup

3. Circle **V** and **v**.

V W W V N V W M V N

v v w v v u w u v w u

Van vet vest never Val very

Instructor's Notes: Introduce the letters *Uu* and *Vv*. Say the letter names. Identify the key pictures. Tell students *umbrella* begins with *u* and *van* begins with *v*. Point out the difference between the capital (upper-case) and small (lower-case) letters. Then read the directions and have students complete the activities.

Ww water  **Xx** ax

1. Write the letters.

2. Circle **W** and **w**.

W M W N W V V W N

w u v w w v u w v v v

wig Will wet win wax Walt

3. Circle **X** and **x**.

X A X V X K K X A K

x w x x v k w x x k v

ax six Rex tax wax box

Yy yell

Zz zipper

1. Write the letters.

Y y

Z z

2. Circle **Y** and **y**.

Y Y K Y I Y K T K Y I

y w y y p g j y q v y

yes yet yell day you very

3. Circle **Z** and **z**.

Z N Z Z M Z E F N Z

z x z z w e v z v w z

jazz zip Liz buzz quiz zigzag

Instructor's Notes: Introduce the letters *Yy* and *Zz*. Say the letter names. Identify the key pictures. Tell students *yell* begins with *y* and *zipper* begins with *z*. Point out the difference between the capital (upper-case) and small (lower-case) letters. Then read the directions and have students complete the activities.

Review Ss, Tt, Uu, Vv, Ww, Xx, Yy, Zz

1. Trace the letters.

S s T t U u V v W w X x Y y Z z

2. Write the letters.

_____

3. Write the missing letters.

_____ U V _____ X _____ Z

s _____ v _____ y

4. Draw lines to match the letters.

S	u	W	x
T	v	X	w
U	t	Y	z
V	s	Z	y

5. Circle the letters.

Ss	sis miss test yes set
Yy	yes yell yam yet very

Instructor's Notes: Review *Ss–Zz* together. Have students make flash cards for these letters. Read the directions. Then help as needed. For students who need extra practice in the alphabet and visual discrimination of letter shapes use Blackline Master 2, and for those needing extra practice in forming letters, use Blackline Master 1 in the *Reading for Today Instructor's Guide.*

Review Aa–Zz

1. Write the missing letters.

A _ _ D _ _ G _ I _ K _ M

N _ P _ _ S _ U _ W _ _ Z

2. Draw lines to match the letters.

B	h	K	r	W	z
F	b	M	q	S	u
C	a	J	k	X	t
H	i	O	m	T	s
D	f	R	l	Z	w
A	g	L	p	V	x
E	c	Q	o	Y	v
I	d	N	n	U	y
G	e	P	j		

Instructor's Notes: Review the capital (upper-case) letters with students. Read the directions together. After students complete the page, give additional practice by asking them to identify letters at random.

1. Write the missing letters.

a b d   g i   l

n o   r t   v   x y

2. Circle the letters.

Gg	get dog Gus egg jog
Rr	Rod rock dirt rag run
Dd	dog bad nod Dot red
Mm	Max miss ham Pam met
Pp	Pam cap pad pen pop
Ff	fit Cliff Fran fax fan
Bb	Bob bell web Bess tab
Qq	quit quick quiz Quinn quiet

Instructor's Notes: Review the small (lower-case) letters with students. Read the directions. After students complete the page, give additional practice by asking them to identify letters at random.

The Alphabet

Aa   Bb   Cc   Dd

Ee   Ff   Gg   Hh

Ii   Jj   Kk   Ll

Mm   Nn   Oo   Pp

Qq   Rr   Ss   Tt

Uu   Vv   Ww

Xx   Yy   Zz

Instructor's Notes: Tell students that this chart shows all upper- and lower-case letters of the alphabet as they are done in printing, or manuscript, style. Point out that when an application or other form they may fill out says "please print," this is the kind of writing they should use.

Aa Bb Cc Dd

Ee Ff Gg Hh

Ii Jj Kk Ll

Mm Nn Oo Pp

Qq Rr Ss Tt

Uu Vv Ww

Xx Yy Zz

Instructor's Notes: Tell students that this chart shows all the upper- and lower-case letters of the alphabet as they are done in handwriting, or cursive, style. Point out that whenever an application or other form they may fill out says "signature," this is the kind of writing they should use to sign their name.

Numbers

Practice writing these numbers.

1 _____	15 _____
2 _____	16 _____
3 _____	17 _____
4 _____	18 _____
5 _____	19 _____
6 _____	20 _____
7 _____	30 _____
8 _____	40 _____
9 _____	50 _____
10 _____	60 _____
11 _____	70 _____
12 _____	80 _____
13 _____	90 _____
14 _____	100 _____

Instructor's Notes: Have students practice writing the numbers. Point out that this list leaves some numbers out, for example 21, 22, etc. If students have difficulty forming the numbers or need extra practice, use Blackline Master 1 in the *Reading for Today Instructor's Guide*.

Write

Fill out the form. Use information about yourself.

City Public Library

Library Card Application

PLEASE PRINT

Name:_____
      (LAST)   (FIRST)   (MIDDLE)

Address:_____
        (NUMBER AND STREET)

_____
(CITY)

_____
(STATE)   (ZIP CODE)

Telephone:_____
          (AREA CODE)   (NUMBER)

Social Security Number:_____

Signature:_____

Instructor's Notes: Talk about what the form is for and the kind of information it requests. Read the parts of the form with students and help them fill in the information. Point out the direction that says "please print." Remind students to use handwriting for their signature.

25

Unit 1

Mm   Money begins with the **m** sound.

A. Write M and m.

M m

B. Write m if you hear the m sound.

1.

2.

3.

4.

m

5.

6.

7.

8.

C. Say a sentence. Your teacher writes it here.

D. Circle the words with M and m. Copy the words.

Instructor's Notes: Tell students the *m* sound is heard at the beginning of *money, machine, May, meat.* Ask for more examples. Read the directions. Review the picture names: 1 man, 2 mat, 3 mop, 4 bed, 5 table, 6 milk, 7 map, 8 mail. For C, have students dictate a sentence using at least one *m* word. Write the sentence. Have students write it in a notebook or journal.

Dd   Dog begins with the **d** sound.

A. Write **D** and **d**.

D d

B. Write **d** if you hear the **d** sound.

1.

2.

3.

4.

5.

6.

7.

8.

C. Say a sentence. Your teacher writes it here.

D. Circle the words with **D** and **d**. Copy the words.

Instructor's Notes: Tell students that the *d* sound is heard at the beginning of *dog, door, date, December*. Ask for more examples. Read the directions. Review the picture names: 1 darts, 2 van, 3 desk, 4 mop, 5 dam, 6 dishes, 7 door, 8 dice. For C, have students dictate a sentence using at least one *d* word. Write the sentence. Have students write it in a notebook or journal.

Ff

Food begins with the **f** sound.

A. Write **F** and **f**.

F f

B. Write **f** if you hear the **f** sound.

1.	2.	3.	4.

_____

5.	6.	7.	8.

_____

C. Say a sentence. Your teacher writes it here.

_____

D. Circle the words with **F** and **f**. Copy the words.

_____

Instructor's Notes: Tell students the *f* sound is heard at the beginning of *food, February, family, face*. Ask for more examples. Read the directions. Review the picture names: 1 fish, 2 mail, 3 feather, 4 football, 5 fan, 6 apple, 7 fork, 8 fuse. For C, have students dictate a sentence using at least one *f* word. Write the sentence. Have students write it in a notebook or journal.

Gg Go begins with the **g** sound.

A. Write **G** and **g**.

G g

B. Write **g** if you hear the **g** sound.

1.

_____

2.

_____

3.

_____

4.

_____

5.

_____

6.

_____

7.

_____

8.

_____

C. Say a sentence. Your teacher writes it here.

_____

D. Circle the words with **G** and **g**. Copy the words.

_____

Instructor's Notes: Tell students the *g* sound is heard at the beginning of *go, gift, garden, gold*. Ask for more examples. Read the directions. Review the picture names: 1 gum, 2 zipper, 3 gate, 4 game, 5 gas, 6 goat, 7 guitar, 8 desk. For C, have students dictate a sentence using at least one *g* word. Write the sentence. Have students write it in a notebook or journal.

ha**m**　　　　be**d**　　　　lea**f**　　　　lo**g**

A. Circle **m**, **d**, **f**, or **g**.

1.

(m) d f

2.

f d g

3.

m f g

4.

g m f

5.

f m g

6.

f m d

7.

g f d

8.

d m g

B. Write the letter you hear.

1. _____　　　　2. _____　　　　3. _____　　　　4. _____

5. da____　　　6. lea____　　　7. do____　　　8. ma____

Instructor's Notes: For A, say the picture names and have students circle the letter for the last sound. For B, 1–4, dictate two words at a time and have students write the letter for the last sound: *ham, gum; dog, flag; lid, bed; leaf, roof.* For B, 5–8, say *dam, leaf, dog, mad* and have students write the letter for the last sound in each word.

Short a Apple begins with the short a sound.

A. Write A and a.

A a

B. Write a if you hear the short a sound.

1.

2.
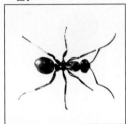

3.

4.

5.

6.

7.

8.

C. Say a sentence. Your teacher writes it here.

D. Circle the words with short a. Copy the words.

Instructor's Notes: Tell students the short *a* sound is heard at the beginning of *apple, at, ax*. Ask for more examples. Read the directions. Review the picture names: 1 animals, 2 ant, 3 ax, 4 key, 5 dishes, 6 astronaut, 7 alligator, 8 apple. For C, have students dictate a sentence using at least one short *a* word. Write the sentence. Have students write it in a notebook or journal.

Short a Man has the short a sound.

A. Write a.

a _____

B. Write a if you hear the short a sound.

1.

2.

3.

4.

_____ _____ _____ _____

5.

6.

7.

8.

_____ _____ _____ _____

C. Say a sentence. Your teacher writes it here.

_____

D. Circle the words with short a. Copy the words.

_____

Instructor's Notes: Tell students the short *a* sound is heard in *man, band, sat, cab*. Ask for more examples. Read the directions. Review the picture names: 1 gas, 2 fan, 3 can, 4 olive, 5 ham, 6 cat, 7 egg, 8 van. For C, have students dictate a sentence using at least one short *a* word. Write the sentence. Have students write it in a notebook or journal.

Review m, d, f, g, a

A. Write **m**, **d**, **f**, **g**, or **a**.

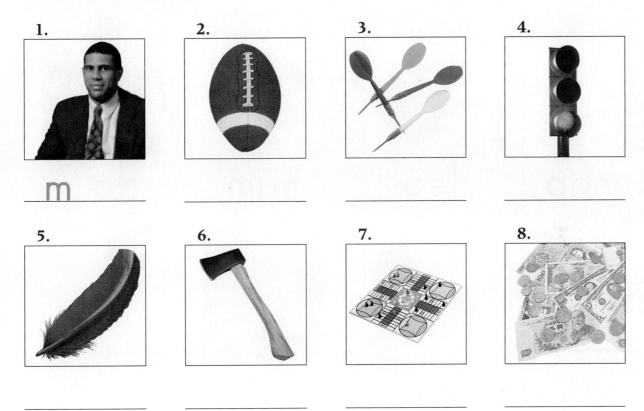

1.
m

2.

3.

4.

5.

6.

7.

8.

B. Circle the word. Write the word.

1.
(map)
gap
tap

map

2.
can
man
fan

3.
bat
cat
mat

Instructor's Notes: Read the directions. Review all picture names: 1 man, 2 football, 3 darts, 4 go, 5 feather, 6 ax, 7 game, 8 money. For A, have students write the letter for the first sound heard in each picture name. For B, have students circle and write the word that names each picture. Complete the first item together.

Review   m, d, f, g, a

Write the letter.

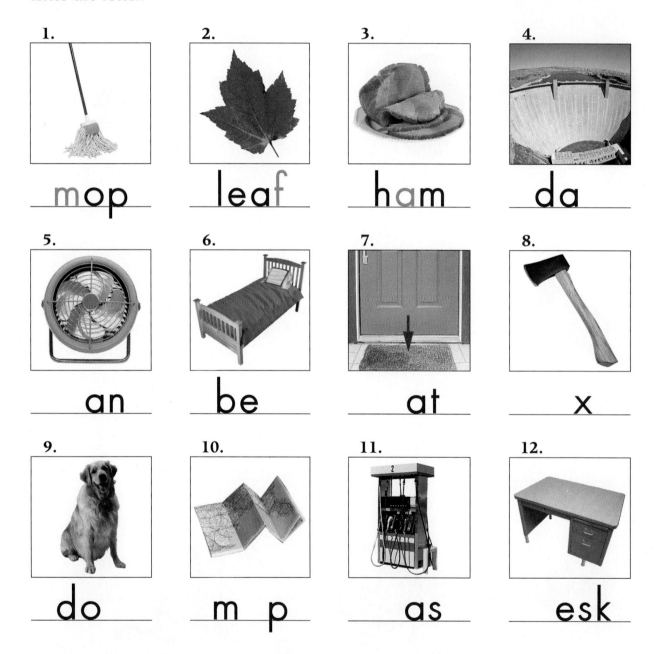

1. __ mop

2. leaf

3. h a m

4. da __

5. __ an

6. be __

7. __ at

8. __ x

9. do __

10. m __ p

11. __ as

12. __ esk

Instructor's Notes: Read the directions. Review the picture names: 1 mop, 2 leaf, 3 ham, 4 dam, 5 fan, 6 bed, 7 mat, 8 ax, 9 dog, 10 map, 11 gas, 12 desk. Have students write the missing letter to finish each word. Complete the first item together.

34

Unit 2

A. Read the words.

dog   money   food   go   ham   bed   leaf   log   apple   man

B. Copy the words.

_____

_____

C. Make up a story. Copy the story.

_____

_____

_____

_____

_____

_____

D. Write a title for your story.

_____

Instructor's Notes: Read the words with students. For C, ask students to make up a story or describe an experience using one or more of the words. Write the story on scratch paper as students dictate it. Have students copy the story and then practice reading it to you.

Bb Bed begins with the **b** sound.

A. Write **B** and **b**.

B b

B. Write **b** if you hear the **b** sound.

1.

2.

3.

4.

_____

5.

6.

7.

8.

_____

C. Say a sentence. Your teacher writes it here.

_____

D. Circle the words with **B** and **b**. Copy the words.

_____

Instructor's Notes: Tell students the *b* sound is heard at the beginning of *bed, binoculars, boat, bee*. Ask for more examples. Read the directions. Review the picture names: 1 belt, 2 bat, 3 map, 4 banana, 5 door, 6 bus, 7 book, 8 button. For C, have students dictate a sentence using at least one *b* word. Write the sentence. Have students write it in a notebook or journal.

Tt Table begins with the **t** sound.

A. Write T and t.

T t

B. Write t if you hear the t sound.

1.
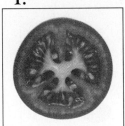

2.

3.

4.

5.

6.

7.

8.

C. Say a sentence. Your teacher writes it here.

D. Circle the words with T and t. Copy the words.

Instructor's Notes: Tell students the *t* sound is heard at the beginning of *table, tea, tax, Tuesday*. Ask for more examples. Read the directions. Review the picture names: 1 tomato, 2 tire, 3 fork, 4 tie, 5 tools, 6 TV, 7 toaster, 8 bed. For C, have students dictate a sentence using at least one *t* word. Write the sentence. Have students write it in a notebook or journal.

Ss Sick begins with the s sound.

A. Write S and s.

S s

B. Write s if you hear the s sound.

1.

2.

3.

4.

5.

6.

7.

8.

C. Say a sentence. Your teacher writes it here.

D. Circle the words with S and s. Copy the words.

Instructor's Notes: Tell students the *s* sound is heard at the beginning of *sick, Sunday, summer, six.* Ask for more examples. Read the directions. Review the picture names: 1 seed, 2 sandwich, 3 six, 4 socks, 5 saw, 6 milk, 7 safe, 8 gate. For C, have students dictate a sentence using at least one *s* word. Write the sentence. Have students write it in a notebook or journal.

Ww Water begins with the w sound.

A. Write W and w.

W w

B. Write w if you hear the w sound.

1.

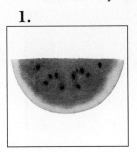

2.

3.

4.

5.

6.

7.

8.

C. Say a sentence. Your teacher writes it here.

D. Circle the words with W and w. Copy the words.

Instructor's Notes: Tell students the *w* sound is heard at the beginning of *water, week, work, Wednesday*. Ask for more examples. Review the picture names: 1 watermelon, 2 book, 3 wallet, 4 watch, 5 woman, 6 window, 7 feather, 8 web. For C, have students dictate a sentence using at least one *w* word. Write the sentence. Have students write it in a notebook or journal.

we**b**

co**t**

bu**s**

A. Circle **b**, **t**, or **s**.

1.

(**b**) t s

2.

b s t

3.

s t b

4.

t s b

5.

s t b

6.

b s t

7.

t s b

8.

b t s

B. Write the letter you hear.

1. _____   2. _____   3. _____   4. _____

5. ye_____   6. ga_____   7. se_____   8. jo_____

Instructor's Notes: For B, 1–4, dictate two words at a time and have students write the letter for the last sound: *jet, hat; cab, tub; dress, bass; sat, get.* For B, 5–8, say *yes, gas, set, job* and have students write the letter for the last sound in each word.

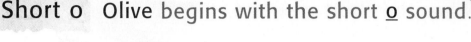

Short o   Olive begins with the short <u>o</u> sound.

A. Write <u>o</u>.

_____

B. Write <u>o</u> if you hear the short <u>o</u> sound.

1.

_____

2.

_____

3.

_____

4.

_____

5.

_____

6.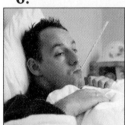

_____

7.

_____

8.

_____

C. Say a sentence. Your teacher writes it here.

_____

D. Circle the words with short <u>o</u>. Copy the words.

_____

Instructor's Notes: Tell students that the short _o_ sound is heard at the beginning of _olive, ox, otter_. Ask for more examples. Read the directions. Review the picture names: 1 olive, 2 tire, 3 ax, 4 otter, 5 October, 6 sick, 7 ostrich, 8 ox. For C, have students dictate a sentence using at least one short _o_ word. Write the sentence. Have students write it in a notebook or journal.

Short o   Box has the short o sound.

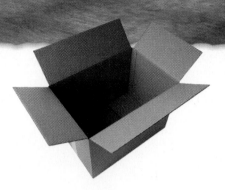

A. Write O and o.

_____

B. Write o if you hear the short o sound.

1.	2.	3.	4.
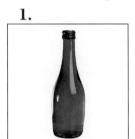			

_____   _____   _____   _____

5.	6.	7.	8.
			STOP

_____   _____   _____   _____

C. Say a sentence. Your teacher writes it here.

_____

_____

D. Circle the words with short o. Copy the words.

_____

Instructor's Notes: Tell students that the short *o* sound is heard in *box*, *spot*, *jog*, *mop*. Ask for more examples. Read the directions. Review the picture names: 1 bottle, 2 socks, 3 cot, 4 can, 5 pot, 6 clock, 7 apple, 8 stop. For C, have students dictate a sentence using at least one short *o* word. Write the sentence. Have students write it in a notebook or journal.

Review   b, t, s, w, o

A. Write <u>b</u>, <u>t</u>, <u>s</u>, <u>w</u>, or <u>o</u>.

1.

_____

2.

_____

3.

_____

4.

_____

5.

_____

6.

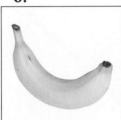

_____

7.

_____

8.

_____

B. Circle the word. Write the word.

1.

 ox
box
fox

_____

2.

pot
lot
got

_____

3.

socks
docks
rocks

_____

Instructor's Notes: Read the directions. Review all picture names: 1 tire, 2 belt, 3 window, 4 sandwich, 5 olive, 6 banana, 7 TV, 8 watch. For A, have students write the letter for the first sound heard in each picture name. For B, have students circle and write the word that names each picture.

Review

Write the letter.

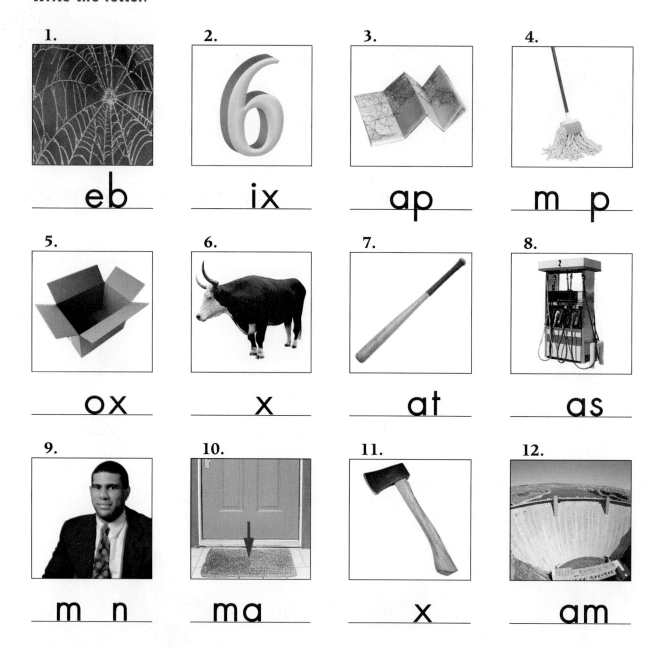

1. _ e b

2. _ i x

3. _ a p

4. m _ p

5. _ o x

6. _ x

7. _ a t

8. _ a s

9. m _ n

10. m a _

11. _ x

12. _ a m

Instructor's Notes: Read the directions. Review the picture names: 1 web, 2 six, 3 map, 4 mop, 5 box, 6 ox, 7 bat, 8 gas. 9 man, 10 mat, 11 ax, 12 dam. Have students write the missing letter to finish each word. Complete the first item together.

Read a Story

Read. Circle the word. Write the word.

1. Bob _____sat_____ at the dam.

bag
(sat)
sad

2. Tom swam to _____.

Tom
dog
Bob

3. Tom _____ a mat and sat by Bob.

mob
got
mad

4. "Is that fog?" _____ asked Tom.

bog
Tom
Bob

5. "That is _____," Tom said to Bob.

got
smog
tag

6. "Smog is _____," said Tom.

bad
mat
boss

Think About It

1. Who sat at the dam?
2. Who asked about the fog?
3. What is bad?

Instructor's Notes: Introduce these sight words: *the, to, a, and, by, is, that, asked, said, from, about*. Explain the use of the *-ed* ending. Then read the directions and answer choices together. In Think About It, introduce the words *who* and *what*. Read the questions together and discuss the answers.

Read and Write

A. Read the words.

bed   table   sick   water   web   cot   bus   olive   box

B. Copy the words.

_____

_____

C. Make up a story. Copy the story.

_____

_____

_____

_____

_____

D. Write a title for your story.

_____

Instructor's Notes: Read the words with students. For C, ask students to make up a story or describe an experience using one or more of the words. Write the story on scratch paper as students dictate it. Have students copy the story and then practice reading it to you.

Kk   Key begins with the **k** sound.

A. Write **K** and **k**.

K k

B. Write **k** if you hear the **k** sound.

1.

2.
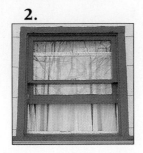

3.

4.

5.
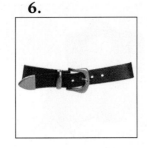

6.

7.

8.

C. Say a sentence. Your teacher writes it here.

D. Circle the words with **K** and **k**. Copy the words.

Instructor's Notes: Tell students the *k* sound is heard at the beginning of *key, kiss, kitchen, ketchup*. Ask for more examples. Read the directions. Review the picture names: 1 kitchen, 2 window, 3 kettle, 4 kite, 5 king, 6 belt, 7 key, 8 kitten. For C, have students dictate a sentence using at least one *k* word. Write the sentence. Have students write it in a notebook or journal.

Jj   Jeep begins with the j̲ sound.

A. Write J̲ and j̲.

J j

B. Write j̲ if you hear the j̲ sound.

1.

2.

3.

4.

5.

6.

7.

8.

C. Say a sentence. Your teacher writes it here.

D. Circle the words with J̲ and j̲. Copy the words.

Instructor's Notes: Tell students the *j* sound is heard at the beginning of *jeep, job, January, jury*. Ask for more examples. Read the directions. Review the picture names: 1 milk, 2 jam, 3 jacket, 4 juice, 5 jet, 6 jar, 7 judge, 8 banana. For C, have students dictate a sentence using at least one *j* word. Write the sentence. Have students write it in a notebook or journal.

Pp   People begins with the p sound.

A. Write P and p.

P p

B. Write p if you hear the p sound.

1.
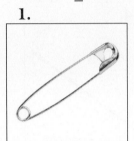

2.

3.
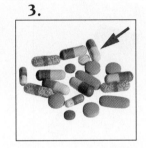

4.

5.

6.

7.

8.
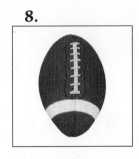

C. Say a sentence. Your teacher writes it here.

D. Circle the words with P and p. Copy the words.

Instructor's Notes: Tell students the *p* sound is heard at the beginning of *people, paper, pencil, picture*. Ask for more examples. Read the directions. Review the picture names: 1 pin, 2 darts, 3 pill, 4 cot, 5 parachute, 6 pencil, 7 pot, 8 football. For C, have students dictate a sentence using at least one *p* word. Write the sentence. Have students write it in a notebook or journal.

Nn   Nurse begins with the n sound.

A. Write N and n.

N n

B. Write n if you hear the n sound.

1.

2.

3.

4.

5.

6.
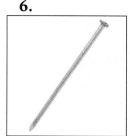

7.
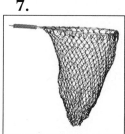

8.

C. Say a sentence. Your teacher writes it here.

D. Circle the words with N and n. Copy the words.

Instructor's Notes: Tell students the *n* sound is heard at the beginning of *nurse, nail, name, north*. Ask for more examples. Read the directions. Review the picture names: 1 newspaper, 2 ax, 3 bat, 4 needle, 5 note, 6 nail, 7 net, 8 nest. For C, have students dictate a sentence using at least one *n* word. Write the sentence. Have students write it in a notebook or journal.

for**k**   mo**p**   va**n**

A. Circle **k**, **p**, or **n**.

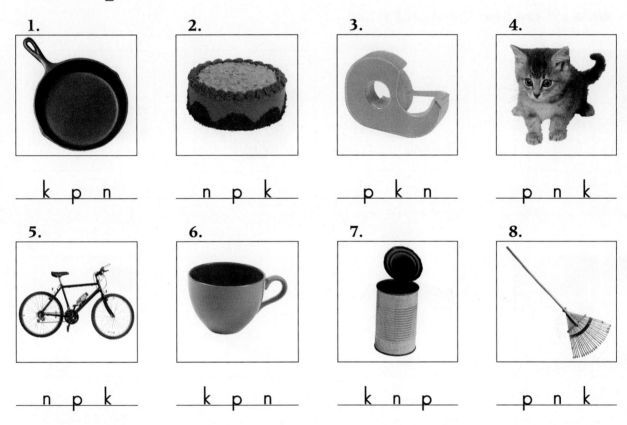

1. _k p n_

2. _n p k_

3. _p k n_

4. _p n k_

5. _n p k_

6. _k p n_

7. _k n p_

8. _p n k_

B. Write the letter you hear.

1. _____   2. _____   3. _____   4. _____

5. ma_____   6. bi___e   7. pi_____   8. jee_____

Instructor's Notes : : For A, say the picture names and have students circle the letter for the last sound. For B, 1–4, dictate two words at a time and have students write the letter for the last sound: *lion, kitten; ketchup, cap; hook, cake; tape, rope.* For B, 5–8, say *map, bike, pin, jeep* and have students write the letter for the last sound in each word.

Short i   **Inch** begins with the short **i** sound.

A. Write **I** and **i**.

I i

B. Write **i** if you hear the short **i** sound.

1.

2.

You're Invited

3.

4.

5.

6.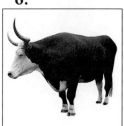

7.

8.

C. Say a sentence. Your teacher writes it here.

D. Circle the words with short **i**. Copy the words.

Instructor's Notes: Tell students the short *i* sound is heard at the beginning of *inch, insect, ill, is*. Ask for more examples. Read the directions. Review the picture names: 1 igloo, 2 invitation, 3 apple, 4 ink, 5 insulation, 6 ox, 7 inch, 8 ax. For C, have students dictate a sentence using at least one short *i* word. Write the sentence. Have students write it in a notebook or journal.

Short i   Mitt has the short i sound.

A. Write i.

i
_____

B. Write i if you hear the short i sound.

1.	2.	3.	4.

_____ _____ _____ _____

5.	6.	7.	8.

_____ _____ _____ _____

C. Say a sentence. Your teacher writes it here.

_____

D. Circle the words with short i. Copy the words.

_____

Review   k, j, p, n, i

A. Write <u>k</u>, <u>j</u>, <u>p</u>, <u>n</u>, or <u>i</u>.

1.

_____

2.

_____

3.

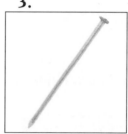

_____

4.

_____

5.

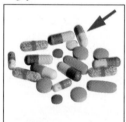

_____

6.

_____

7.

_____

8.

_____

B. Circle the word. Write the word.

1.

win
fin
pin

_____

2.

kick
sick
pick

_____

3.

mitt
kit
sit

_____

Review

Write the letter.

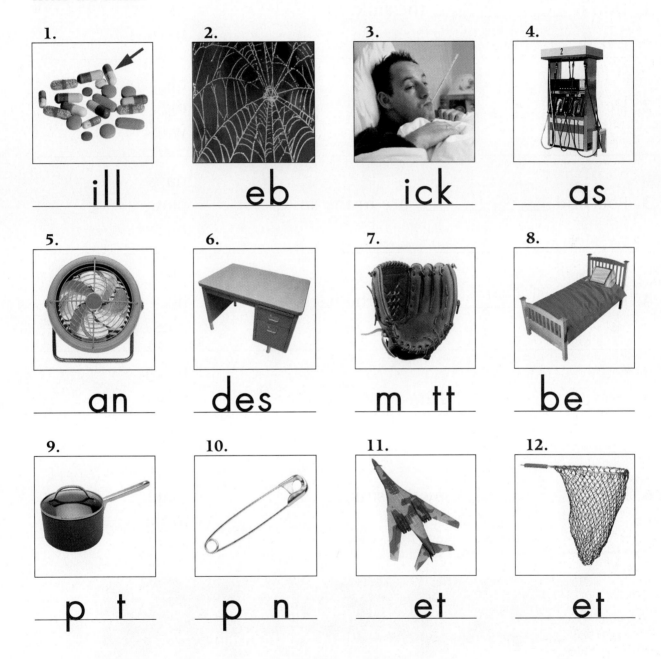

1. i l l

2. _ e b

3. _ ick

4. _ as

5. _ an

6. des_

7. m _ tt

8. be_

9. p _ t

10. p _ n

11. _ et

12. _ et

Instructor's Notes: Read the directions. Review the picture names: 1 pill, 2 web, 3 sick, 4 gas, 5 fan, 6 desk, 7 mitt, 8 bed, 9 pot, 10 pin, 11 jet, 12 net. Have students write the missing letter to finish each word. Complete the first item together.

55

Unit 2

Read a Story

Read. Circle the word. Write the word.

1. Don is _____ the sink.

    cat
    at
    mad

2. He has a _____ job.

    big
    dig
    wag

3. Pots and _____ are in the sink.

    naps
    pans
    pigs

4. Pam _____ Don on the back.

    pits
    pots
    pats

5. Don _____ Pam a mop.

    hands
    hints
    has

6. Pam _____ by the sink.

    mats
    maps
    mops

Think About It

1. Who is at the sink?
2. What is in the sink?
3. Where does Pam mop?

Instructor's Notes: Introduce these sight words: *is, the, has, a, and, are, by*. Explain the use of the *-s* ending. Then read the directions and answer choices together. In Think About It, introduce the words *who, what,* and *where*. Read the questions together and discuss the answers.

A. Read the words.

key   jeep   people   nurse   fork   mop   van   inch   mitt

B. Copy the words.

_____

_____

C. Make up a story. Copy the story.

_____

_____

_____

_____

_____

D. Write a title for your story.

_____

Instructor's Notes: Read the words with students. For C, ask students to make up a story or describe an experience using one or more of the words. Write the story on scratch paper as students dictate it. Have students copy the story and then practice reading it to you.

57

Unit 2

Cc Car begins with the c sound.

A. Write C and c.

C c

B. Write c if you hear the c sound.

1.	2.	3.	4.

5.	6.	7.	8.

C. Say a sentence. Your teacher writes it here.

D. Circle the words with C and c. Copy the words.

Instructor's Notes: Tell students the *c* sound is heard at the beginning of *car, copy, Canada, coffee*. Ask for more examples. Read the directions. Review the picture names: 1 cap, 2 cake, 3 cot, 4 otter, 5 cub, 6 cup, 7 cat, 8 table. For C, have students dictate a sentence using at least one *c* word. Write the sentence. Have students write it in a notebook or journal.

Hh   Home begins with the h sound.

A. Write H and h.

H h

B. Write h if you hear the h sound.

1.

_____

2.

_____

3.

_____

4.

_____

5.

_____

6.
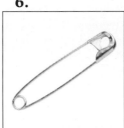

_____

7.
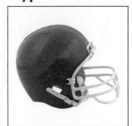

_____

8.

_____

C. Say a sentence. Your teacher writes it here.

_____

D. Circle the words with H and h. Copy the words.

_____

Instructor's Notes: Tell students the *h* sound is heard at the beginning of *home, help, hammer, heart.* Ask for more examples. Read the directions. Review the picture names: 1 hat, 2 hive, 3 king, 4 hole, 5 hose, 6 pin, 7 helmet, 8 hug. For C, have students dictate a sentence using at least one *h* word. Write the sentence. Have students write it in a notebook or journal.

Ll Light begins with the l sound.

A. Write L and l.

L l

B. Write l if you hear the l sound.

1.

2.

3.

4.

5.

6.

7.

8.

C. Say a sentence. Your teacher writes it here.

D. Circle the words with L and l. Copy the words.

Instructor's Notes: Tell students the *l* sound is heard at the beginning of *light, lease, learn, lottery*. Ask for more examples. Read the directions. Review the picture names: 1 water, 2 ladder, 3 log, 4 leaf, 5 lock, 6 mop, 7 letter, 8 lid. For C, have students dictate a sentence using at least one *l* word. Write the sentence. Have students write it in a notebook or journal.

Rr   Radio begins with the r sound.

A. Write **R** and **r**.

R r

B. Write **r** if you hear the **r** sound.

1.

2.

3.

4.

5.

6.

7.

8.
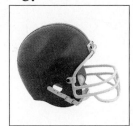

C. Say a sentence. Your teacher writes it here.

D. Circle the words with **R** and **r**. Copy the words.

Instructor's Notes: Tell students the *r* sound is heard at the beginning of *radio, read, refund, rain*. Ask for more examples. Read the directions. Review the picture names: 1 rake, 2 robe, 3 rod, 4 rope, 5 mat, 6 rose, 7 rug, 8 helmet. For C, have students dictate a sentence using at least one *r* word. Write the sentence. Have students write it in a notebook or journal.

Short u   **Umbrella** begins with the short **u** sound.

A. Write **U** and **u**.

U u

B. Write **u** if you hear the short **u** sound.

1.

2.

3.

4.
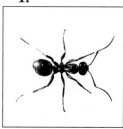

5.
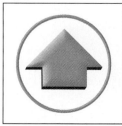

6.

7.

8.

C. Say a sentence. Your teacher writes it here.

D. Circle the words with short **u**. Copy the words.

Instructor's Notes: Tell students the short *u* sound is heard at the beginning of *umbrella, uncle, up.* Ask for more examples. Read the directions. Review the picture names: 1 under, 2 umpire, 3 inch, 4 ant, 5 up, 6 rose, 7 olive, 8 umbrella. For C, have students dictate a sentence using at least one short *u* word. Write the sentence. Have students write it in a notebook or journal.

Short u   Cup has the short <u>u</u> sound.

A. Write <u>u</u>.

u

B. Write <u>u</u> if you hear the short <u>u</u> sound.

1.

2.

3.

4.

5.

6.

7.

8.

C. Say a sentence. Your teacher writes it here.

D. Circle the words with short <u>u</u>. Copy the words.

Instructor's Notes: Tell students the short *u* sound is heard in *cup, lunch, study, clutch*. Ask for more examples. Read the directions. Review the picture names: 1 tub, 2 cat, 3 hug, 4 rug, 5 gum, 6 cub, 7 belt, 8 sun. For C, have students dictate a sentence using at least one short *u* word. Write the sentence. Have students write it in a notebook or journal.

Review c, h, l, r, u

A. Write c, h, l, r, or u.

1.

_____

2.

_____

3.

_____

4.

_____

5.

_____

6.

_____

7.

_____

8.

_____

B. Circle the word. Write the word.

1.

hug
bug
rug
_____

2.

sun
fun
run
_____

3.

cub
tub
rub
_____

Instructor's Notes: Read the directions. Review all picture names: 1 ladder, 2 helmet, 3 umbrella, 4 rake, 5 under, 6 radio, 7 lid, 8 car. For A, have students write the letter for the first sound heard in each picture name. For B, have students circle and write the word that names each picture.

64

Unit 2

Review

Write the letter.

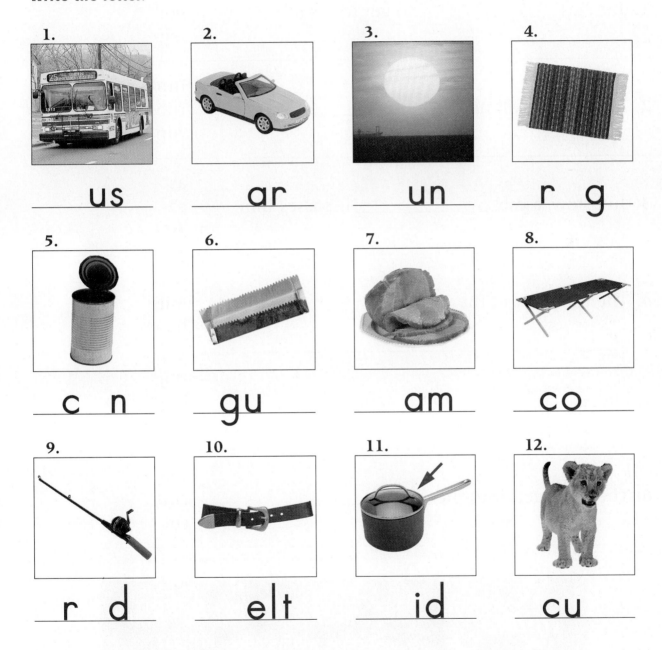

1. us ___

2. ___ ar

3. ___ un

4. r ___ g

5. c ___ n

6. gu ___

7. ___ am

8. co ___

9. r ___ d

10. ___ elt

11. ___ id

12. cu ___

Instructor's Notes: Read the directions. Review the picture names: 1 bus, 2 car, 3 sun, 4 rug, 5 can, 6 gum, 7 ham, 8 cot, 9 rod, 10 belt, 11 lid, 12 cub. Have students write the missing letter to finish each word. Complete the first item together.

Read a Story

Read. Circle the word. Write the word.

1. Jud has _____ to get to his job.

   not
   got
   log

2. But his car will not _____ .

   fun
   rub
   run

3. Jud stops a cab _____ it passes him.

   as
   ax
   at

4. The cab stops at the top of the _____ .

   pill
   hill
   ham

5. Jud _____ to the cab.

   rugs
   hugs
   runs

6. Then Jud gets into the _____ .

   cab
   cub
   cot

Think About It

1. Who has a car that will not run?
2. How will he get to his job?
3. Where does the cab stop?

Instructor's Notes: Introduce these sight words: *to, his, of, the, then, into*. Explain the use of the *-s* and *-es* endings. Then read the directions and answer choices together. In Think About It, introduce the words *who, how,* and *where*. Read the questions together and discuss the answers.

66

Unit 2

Read and Write

A. Read the words.

car   home   light   radio   umbrella   cup

B. Copy the words.

_____

_____

C. Make up a story. Copy the story.

_____

_____

_____

_____

_____

D. Write a title for your story.

_____

Instructor's Notes: Read the words with students. For C, ask students to make up a story or describe an experience using one or more of the words. Write the story on scratch paper as students dictate it. Have students copy the story and then practice reading it to you.

Vv   Van begins with the **v** sound.

A. Write **V** and **v**.

V v

B. Write **v** if you hear the **v** sound.

1.

2.

3.

4.

5.

6.

7.

8.

C. Say a sentence. Your teacher writes it here.

D. Circle the words with **V** and **v**. Copy the words.

Instructor's Notes: Tell students the *v* sound is heard at the beginning of *van, visit, vote, valentine*. Ask for more examples. Read the directions. Review the picture names: 1 letter, 2 vase, 3 vet, 4 vegetables, 5 volcano, 6 wallet, 7 van, 8 vine. For C, have students dictate a sentence using at least one *v* word. Write the sentence. Have students write it in a notebook or journal.

Y y   Yell begins with the **y** sound.

A. Write **Y** and **y**.

B. Write **y** if you hear the **y** sound.

1.

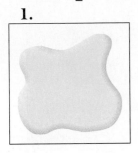

2.

3.

4.

5.

6.

7.

YIELD

8.

C. Say a sentence. Your teacher writes it here.

D. Circle the words with **Y** and **y**. Copy the words.

Instructor's Notes: Tell students the *y* sound is heard at the beginning of *yell, yard, yes, yolk.*
Ask for more examples. Read the directions. Review the picture names: 1 yellow, 2 can,
3 robe, 4 yoyo, 5 yell, 6 yard, 7 yield, 8 yarn. For C, have students dictate a sentence using at
least one *y* word. Write the sentence. Have students write it in a notebook or journal.

Zz Zipper begins with the z sound.

A. Write Z and z.

Z z

B. Write z if you hear the z sound.

1.

2.

3.

4.

5.

6.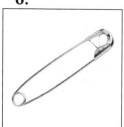

7.

8.

C. Say a sentence. Your teacher writes it here.

D. Circle the words with Z and z. Copy the words.

Instructor's Notes: Tell students the z sound is heard at the beginning of *zipper, zone, zoo, zip.* Ask for more examples. Read the directions. Review the picture names: 1 zipper, 2 zoo, 3 zip code, 4 volcano, 5 zebra, 6 pin, 7 zero, 8 juice. For C, have students dictate a sentence using at least one z word. Write the sentence. Have students write it in a notebook or journal.

Qu qu Quarter begins with the <u>qu</u> sound.

A. Write **Qu** and **qu**.

Qu qu

B. Write **qu** if you hear the **qu** sound.

1.

2.

3.

4.

5.

6.

7.

8.

C. Say a sentence. Your teacher writes it here.

D. Circle the words with **Qu** and **qu**. Copy the words.

Instructor's Notes: Tell students *q* always appears with *u* and the *qu* sound is heard at the beginning of *quarter, question, quiz, quake*. Read the directions. Review the picture names: 1 zip code, 2 quilt, 3 quarterback, 4 queen, 5 van, 6 quarter, 7 rod, 8 quart. For C, have students dictate a sentence using one *qu* word. Write the sentence. Have students write it in a notebook or journal.

71

Unit 2

Xx Ax ends with the **x** sound.

A. Write **X** and **x**.

X x

B. Write **x** if you hear the **x** sound.

1.

2.

3.

4.

5.

6.

7.

8.

C. Say a sentence. Your teacher writes it here.

D. Circle the words with **x**. Copy the words.

Instructor's Notes: Tell students the *x* sound is heard at the end of *ax, tax, fix, complex*. Ask for more examples. Read the directions. Review the picture names: 1 six, 2 fox, 3 ax, 4 can, 5 box, 6 food, 7 wax, 8 tax. For C, have students dictate a sentence using at least one *x* word. Write the sentence. Have students write it in a notebook or journal.

nail   five   ax

A. Circle l, v, or x.

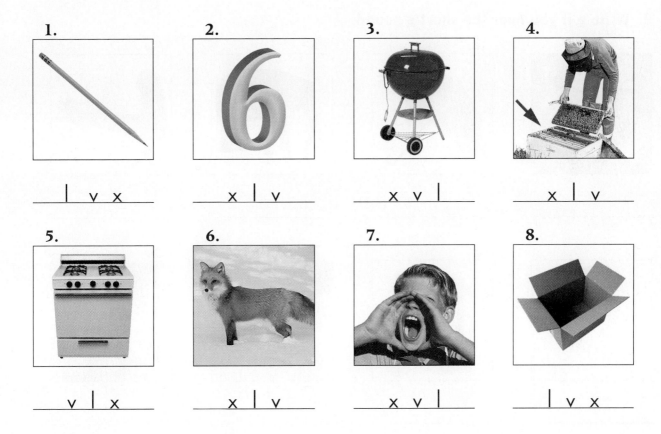

1.

_____ l v x _____

2.

_____ x l v _____

3.

_____ x v l _____

4.

_____ x l v _____

5.

_____ v l x _____

6.

_____ x l v _____

7.

_____ x v l _____

8.

_____ l v x _____

B. Write the letter you hear.

1. _____   2. _____   3. _____   4. _____

5. fi____e   6. ta____   7. mi____   8. unti____

Instructor's Notes: : For A, say the picture names and have students circle the letter for the last sound. For B, 1–4, dictate two words at a time and have students write the letter for the last sound: *wax, index; love, move; sell, meal; give, have.* For B, 5–8, say *five, tax, mix, until.* Have students write the letter for the last sound in each word.

Short e   Egg begins with the short <u>e</u> sound.

A. Write <u>E</u> and <u>e</u>.

E e
_____

B. Write <u>e</u> if you hear the short <u>e</u> sound.

1.
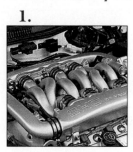

2.

3.
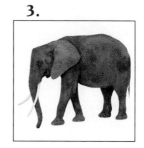

4.
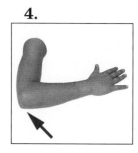

_____   _____   _____   _____

5.

6.

7.

8.

_____   _____   _____   _____

C. Say a sentence. Your teacher writes it here.

_____

D. Circle the words with short <u>e</u>. Copy the words.

_____

Instructor's Notes: Tell students the short *e* sound is heard at the beginning of *egg, energy, enter*. Ask for more examples. Read the directions. Review the picture names: 1 engine, 2 umbrella, 3 elephant, 4 elbow, 5 flag, 6 exit, 7 igloo, 8 elevator. For C, have students dictate a sentence using at least one short *e* word. Write the sentence. Have students write it in a notebook or journal.

Short e   Desk has the short e̱ sound.

A. Write e̱.

e

_____

B. Write e̱ if you hear the short e̱ sound.

1.

_____

2.

_____

3.

_____

4.

_____

5.

_____

6.

_____

7.

_____

8.

_____

C. Say a sentence. Your teacher writes it here.

_____

D. Circle the words with short e̱. Copy the words.

_____

Instructor's Notes: Tell students the short *e* sound is heard in *desk, left, spell, tent*. Ask for more examples. Read the directions. Review the picture names: 1 belt, 2 cat, 3 net, 4 dress, 5 vet, 6 men, 7 nest, 8 bus. For C, have students dictate a sentence using at least one short *e* word. Write the sentence. Have students write it in a notebook or journal.

Review v, y, z, qu, x, e

A. Write <u>v</u>, <u>y</u>, <u>z</u>, <u>qu</u>, or <u>e</u>.

1.

_____

2.

_____

3.

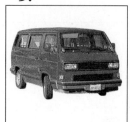

_____

4.

_____

5.

_____

6.

_____

7.

_____

8.

_____

B. Circle the word. Write the word.

1.

wet

vet

bet

_____

2.

fed

red

bed

_____

3.

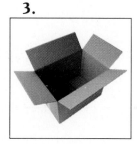

ox

box

fox

_____

Instructor's Notes: Read the directions. Review all picture names: 1 yell, 2 quilt, 3 van, 4 yarn, 5 quarterback, 6 zip code, 7 zoo, 8 volcano. For A, have students write the letter for the first sound heard in each picture name. For B, have students circle and write the word that names each picture.

Review

Write the letter or letters.

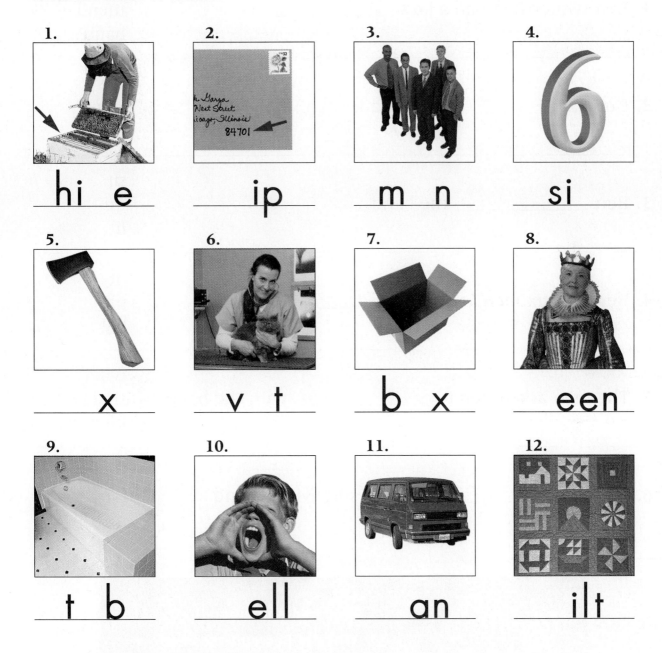

1. hi __ e

2. __ ip

3. m __ n

4. si __

5. __ x

6. __ v t

7. b __ x

8. __ een

9. t __ b

10. __ ell

11. __ an

12. __ ilt

Read a Story

Read. Circle the word. Write the word.

1. Last winter Ben had a jazz _____.

lend
mend
band

_____

2. But jazz _____ be sad.

cat
can
man

_____

3. Ben _____ the band.

sit
quit
lit

_____

4. Ben met six men at a _____ club.

dig
pig
big

_____

5. The men asked Ben to _____ with the band.

wing
sing
king

_____

6. It is _____ for Ben to sing with a band.

fun
fan
fin

Think About It

1. Who had a jazz band?
2. Why did Ben quit the band?
3. What does Ben do at the club?

Instructor's Notes: Introduce these sight words: *winter, a, be, to, the, do, does*. Then read the directions and answer choices together. In Think About It, introduce the words *who, why,* and *what*. Read the questions together and discuss the answers.

Read and Write

A. Read the words.

van   yell   zipper   quarter   ax   nail   five   egg   desk

B. Copy the words.

_____

_____

C. Make up a story. Copy the story.

_____

_____

_____

_____

_____

D. Write a title for your story.

_____

Instructor's Notes: Read the words with students. For C, ask students to make up a story or describe an experience using one or more of the words. Write the story on scratch paper as students dictate it. Have students copy the story and then practice reading it to you.

Unit 2 Review

A. Write the letter.

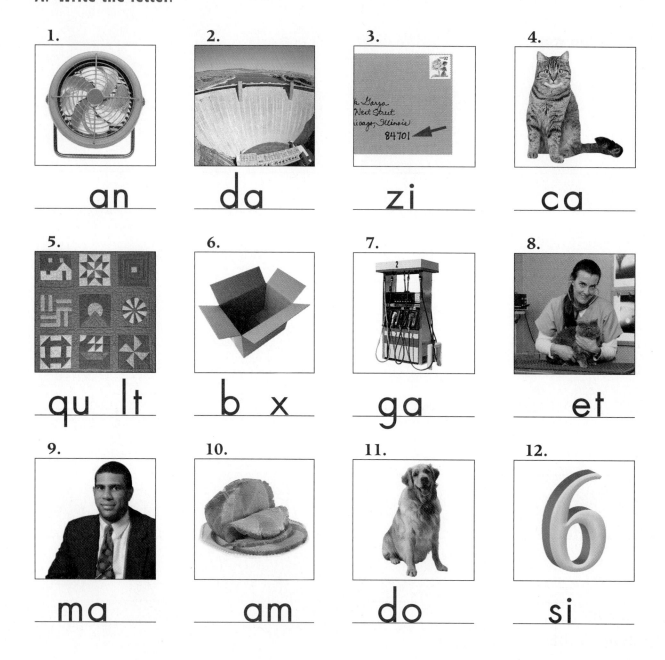

1. an

2. da

3. zi

4. ca

5. qu lt

6. b x

7. ga

8. et

9. ma

10. am

11. do

12. si

Instructor's Notes: Read the directions. Review all picture names: 1 fan, 2 dam, 3 zip code, 4 cat, 5 quilt, 6 box, 7 gas, 8 vet, 9 man, 10 ham, 11 dog, 12 six. Have students write the missing letter to complete each word.

B. Write the letter.

1. at

2. j t

3. c p

4. x

5. eb

6. am

7. ell

8. an

9. be

10. oo

11. ing

12. ug

Instructor's Notes: Read the directions. Review all picture names: 1 bat, 2 jet, 3 cup, 4 ax, 5 web, 6 jam, 7 yell, 8 can, 9 bed, 10 zoo, 11 king, 12 rug. Have students write the missing letter to complete each word.

Long a   Tape has the long <u>a</u> sound.

A. Write tape.

<u>tape</u>

B. Write <u>a</u> if you hear the long <u>a</u> sound.

1.

2.

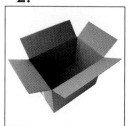

3.

4.

5.

6.

7.

8.

C. Say a sentence. Your teacher writes it here.

D. Circle the words with long <u>a</u>. Copy the words.

Instructor's Notes: Tell students the long *a* sound is heard in *tape, lake, grape, state*. Use *tape* to explain the Consonant + Vowel + Consonant + *e* (CVC + *e*) pattern. Review all picture names: 1 cake, 2 box, 3 gate, 4 safe, 5 inch, 6 game, 7 rake, 8 cage. For C, have students dictate a sentence using one long *a* word. Write the sentence. Have students write it in a notebook or journal.

Short a and Long a

man

tape

A. Circle the word. Write the word.

1.

_____

fin   fan

2.

_____

bet   bat

3.

_____

cat   cot

B. Circle the word. Write the word.

1.
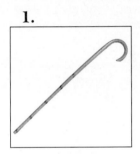

_____

can   cane

2.

_____

tap   tape

3.
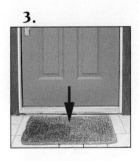

_____

mate   mat

4.

_____

man   mane

5.

_____

cape   cap

6.

_____

vane   van

Instructor's Notes: Read the directions. Review all picture names and word choices: A. 1 fin, 2 bat, 3 cot; B. 1 cane, 2 tape, 3 mat, 4 man, 5 cape, 6 vane. Explain that part A reviews the short *a* sound. Then use *tape* to explain the CVC + *e* pattern. Explain that in part B, students will choose between short *a* and long *a* sounds. Complete the first item together.

Long i Bike has the long i sound.

A. Write bike.

_bike_____

B. Write i if you hear the long i sound.

1.

_____

2.

_____

3.

_____

4.

_____

5.

_____

6.

_____

7.

_____

8.

_____

C. Say a sentence. Your teacher writes it here.

_____

D. Circle the words with long i. Copy the words.

_____

Instructor's Notes: Tell students the long *i* sound is heard in *bike, wife, time, mile*. Use *bike* to explain the CVC + *e* pattern. Read the directions. Review the picture names: 1 bed, 2 dime, 3 rice, 4 kite, 5 dice, 6 pine, 7 vine, 8 five. For C, have students dictate a sentence using at least one long *i* word. Write the sentence. Have students write it in a notebook or journal.

Short i and Long i

 mitt

 bike

A. Circle the word. Write the word.

1.

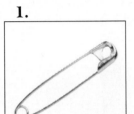

_____

pin   pan

2.

_____

dim   dam

3.

_____

dog   dig

B. Circle the word. Write the word.

1.

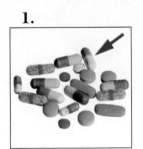

_____

pill   pile

2.

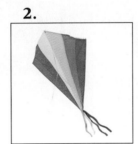

_____

kite   kit

3.

_____

dim   dime

4.

_____

fin   fine

5.

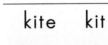

_____

wine   win

6.

_____

fill   file

Instructor's Notes: Read the directions. Review all picture names and word choices: A. 1 pin, 2 dam, 3 dog; B. 1 pill, 2 kite, 3 dime, 4 fin, 5 win, 6 file. Explain that part A reviews the short *i* sound. Then use *bike* to explain the CVC + *e* pattern. Explain that in part B students will choose between short *i* and long *i* sounds. Complete the first item together.

Review Long a and Long i

A. Write a or i.

1.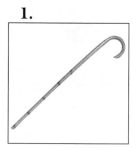

2.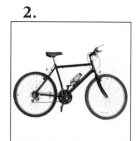

3.

4.

5.

6.

7.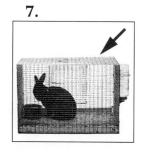

8.

B. Circle the word. Write the word.

1.

cake

bake

rake

2.

file

mile

tile

3.

gate

date

late

Instructor's Notes: Read the directions. Review all picture names and word choices: A. 1 cane, 2 bike, 3 cake, 4 safe, 5 hive, 6 vine, 7 cage, 8 rice; B. 1 rake, 2 file 3 gate. For A, have students write the letter for the long vowel sound heard in each picture name. For B, have students circle and write the word that names each picture.

Read a Story

Read. Circle the word. Write the word.

1. The time is ten past _____.

five
fine
hive

_____

2. Mike and Kate go on a _____.

bat
gate
date

_____

3. They _____ to go to the lake.

lid
like
line

_____

4. They take a bike _____ to the lake.

ride
rid
rake

_____

5. They are safe as they ride in the bike _____.

late
land
lane

_____

6. Mike and Kate like to _____ their time as they ride.

tack
take
time

Think About it

1. What time is it?
2. Who is going on a date?
3. How do they get to the lake?

Instructor's Notes: Introduce these sight words: *go, going, a, they, are, to, the, their.* Then read the directions and answer choices together. In Think About It, introduce the words *who, what,* and *how.* Read the questions together and discuss the answers.

Read and Write

A. Read the words.

tape   kite   bike   cane   fine   cape

B. Copy the words.

_____

_____

C. Make up a story. Copy the story.

_____

_____

_____

_____

_____

D. Write a title for your story.

_____

Instructor's Notes: Read the words with students. For C, ask students to make up a story or describe an experience using one or more of the words. Write the story on scratch paper as students dictate it. Have students copy the story and then practice reading it to you.

Long o   Robe has the long <u>o</u> sound.

A. Write robe.

<u>robe</u>

B. Write <u>o</u> if you hear the long <u>o</u> sound.

1.

2.

3.

4.

5.

6.
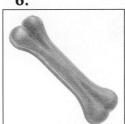

7.

8.

C. Say a sentence. Your teacher writes it here.

_____

D. Circle the words with long <u>o</u>. Copy the words.

_____

Instructor's Notes: Tell students the long *o* sound is heard in *robe, zone, joke, home*. Use *robe* to explain the CVC + *e* pattern. Read the directions. Review the picture names: 1 hose, 2 tote bag, 3 globe, 4 rope, 5 smoke, 6 bone, 7 hole, 8 stove. For C, have students dictate a sentence using at least one long *o* word. Write the sentence. Have students write it in a notebook or journal.

Short o and Long o b<u>o</u>x

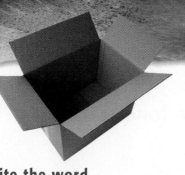

r<u>o</u>be

A. Circle the word. Write the word.

1.

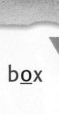

_____

lock   luck

2.

_____

cat   cot

3.

_____

pot   pit

B. Circle the word. Write the word.

1.

_____

mop   mope

2.

EXAM
TUESDAY
4 pm!

_____

note   not

3.

_____

rod   rode

4.

_____

rob   rope

5.

_____

tot   tote

6.

_____

cone   con

Instructor's Notes: Read the directions. Review all picture names and word choices: A. 1 lock, 2 cot, 3 pot; B. 1 mop, 2 note, 3 rod, 4 rope, 5 tote bag, 6 cone. Explain that part A reviews the short o sound. Then use *robe* to explain the CVC + *e* pattern. Explain that in part B, students will choose between short *o* and long *o* sounds. Complete the first item together.

Long u   Mule has the long <u>u</u> sound.

A. Write mule.

mule

B. Write <u>u</u> if you hear the long <u>u</u> sound.

1.
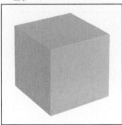

2.

3.

4.

5.

6.

7.

8.

C. Say a sentence. Your teacher writes it here.

D. Circle the words with long <u>u</u>. Copy the words.

Instructor's Notes: Tell students the long *u* sound is heard in *mule, prune, June*. Use *mule* to explain the CVC + e pattern. Read the directions. Review the picture names: 1 cube, 2 tube, 3 fuse, 4 safe, 5 June, 6 tune, 7 dice, 8 flute. For C, have students dictate a sentence using at least one long *u* word. Write the sentence. Have students write it in a notebook or journal.

91

Unit 3

Short u and Long u

cup

mule

A. Circle the word. Write the word.

1.

_____

hug   hog

2.

_____

bed   bud

3.

_____

rug   rag

B. Circle the word. Write the word.

1.

_____

tube   tub

2.

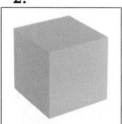

_____

cub   cube

3.

_____

tan   tune

4.

_____

cube   cub

5.

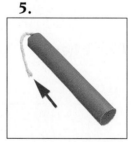

_____

fuss   fuse

6.

_____

cut   cute

Review Long o and Long u

A. Write o or u.

1.
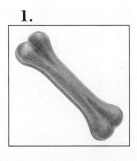

2.

3.

4.

5.

6.

7.

8.

B. Circle the word. Write the word.

1.

tube

rude

cube

2.

hose

nose

rose

3.

pole

hole

mole

Instructor's Notes: Read the directions. Review all picture names and word choices: A. 1 bone, 2 rose, 3 flute, 4 tube, 5 June, 6 stove, 7 mule, 8 rope; B. 1 cube, 2 hose, 3 hole. For A, have students write the letter for the long vowel sound heard in each picture name. For B, have students circle and write the word that names each picture.

Read a Story

Read. Circle the word. Write the word.

1. June is at _____.

hum
home
hive

_____

2. She has on a blue _____.

rob
ride
robe

_____

3. She picks up a _____ in a vase.

rude
rose
rise

_____

4. She smells it with her _____.

nose
name
not

_____

5. Then _____ makes lunch.

Jake
Jim
June

_____

6. June hums a _____ as she makes lunch.

zone
tune
tame

Think About It

1. **Where is June?**

2. **What is in the vase?**

3. **When does June hum?**

Instructor's Notes: Introduce these sight words: *she, a, with, her, then, to*. Explain the *-s* ending. Then read the directions and answer choices together. In Think About It, introduce the words *where, what,* and *when*. Read the questions together and discuss the answers.

Read and Write

A. Read the words.

robe   home   mule   hole   rode   tube

B. Copy the words.

_____

_____

C. Make up a story. Copy the story.

_____

_____

_____

_____

_____

D. Write a title for your story.

_____

Instructor's Notes: Read the words with students. For C, ask students to make up a story or describe an experience using one or more of the words. Write the story on scratch paper as students dictate it. Have students copy the story and then practice reading it to you.

Long e   Leaf and bee have the long e sound.

A. Write leaf and bee.

leaf   bee
_____

B. Write e if you hear the long e sound.

1.

_____

2.

_____

3.
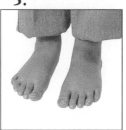
_____

4.

_____

5.

_____

6.
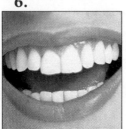
_____

7.

_____

8.

_____

C. Say a sentence. Your teacher writes it here.

_____

D. Circle the words with ea or ee. Copy the words.

_____

Instructor's Notes: Tell students the long *e* sound is heard in *leaf, meat, clean, street, green*. Ask for more examples. Read the directions. Review the picture names: 1 jeans, 2 jeep, 3 feet, 4 beet, 5 seal, 6 teeth, 7 weed, 8 tree. For C, have students dictate a sentence using at least one long *e* word. Write the sentence. Have students write it in a notebook or journal.

Short e and Long e

d<u>e</u>sk  l<u>ea</u>f  b<u>ee</u>

A. Circle the word. Write the word.

1.

_____

jet   jot

2.

_____

nut   net

3.

_____

bad   bed

B. Circle the word. Write the word.

1.

pet   peas

2.

tam   team

3.

set   sea

4.

_____

bet   beet

5.

_____

tea   tax

6.

_____

meat   met

Review Long e

Circle the word. Write the word.

1.

bed
beans
beet

_____

2.

mat
met
meat

_____

3.

tent
tire
tree

_____

4.

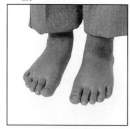

feet
fell
fate

_____

5.

jeans
jeep
jet

_____

6.

bit
belt
bee

_____

7.

seal
sell
sale

_____

8.

weed
wed
win

_____

9.

leaf
left
lean

_____

Instructor's Notes: Read the directions. Review all picture names and word choices: 1 beet,
2 meat, 3 tree, 4 feet, 5 jeep, 6 bee, 7 seal, 8 weed, 9 leaf. Have students circle and write
the word that names each picture.

Read a Story

Read. Circle the word. Write the word.

1. Jean is on a bike _____.

    team
    time
    tame

2. This _____ they eat at Jean's home.

    wake
    week
    wet

3. Jean makes a huge _____to feed the team.

    make
    mile
    meal

4. She grills lean _____ and makes baked beans.

    bike
    beef
    fed

5. The team helps Jean fix the _____.

    meat
    mean
    met

6. Next week they will _____ at Lee's home.

    eat
    egg
    ice

Think About It

1. Who is on a bike team?
2. Where does the team eat this week?
3. What does Jean make for the team to eat?

Instructor's Notes: Introduce these sight words: *a, this, they, to, the,* and, *does*. Discuss the use of *'s* to show the possessive. Then read the directions and answer choices together. In Think About It, introduce the words *who, where,* and *what*. Read the questions together and discuss the answers.

Read and Write

A. Read the words.

leaf   bee   weed   eat   jeep   beans

B. Copy the words.

_____

_____

C. Make up a story. Copy the story.

_____

_____

_____

_____

_____

D. Write a title for your story.

_____

Instructor's Notes: Read the words with students. For C, ask students to make up a story or describe an experience using one or more of the words. Write the story on scratch paper as students dictate it. Have students copy the story and then practice reading it to you.

The Big Game

Joe and his wife Sue have a child named Dean.
Dean has a big game at nine. Joe, Sue, and Dean
want to get up at seven. But Joe and Sue wake up
late. Sue runs to wake Dean. Joe fills the tub for
Dean. A pipe in the tub leaks. Joe and Sue must
mop up the huge mess.

Sue, Joe, and Dean want to have a bite to eat.
But the milk is bad. They do not have time to get
more milk. So they cannot eat until after the game.

Joe, Sue, and Dean get in the van. They want to
get to the game at nine. But the van will not run.
Joe gets a pal to take them to the game. They get
to the game just in time.

Instructor's Notes: Read the title together. Ask students to think about the title and picture
and predict what the story might be about. Then introduce these sight words: *have, a, child,*
want, to, for, they, more, so, do. Then have students read the story.

Think About It

1. Who is Sue?

_____

2. What does Dean have to do at nine?

_____

3. When do Sue, Joe, and Dean want to get up?

_____

4. Why is there a huge mess by the tub?

_____

5. How do Joe, Sue, and Dean get to the big game?

_____

Talk About It

Have you ever had a day like this?

Instructor's Notes: For Think About It, review the words _who, what, when, why, how_. Read the questions together and discuss. Help students write answers. Talk About It can be used as a discussion or writing activity.

Unit 3 Review

A. Write a, ee, i, o, or u.

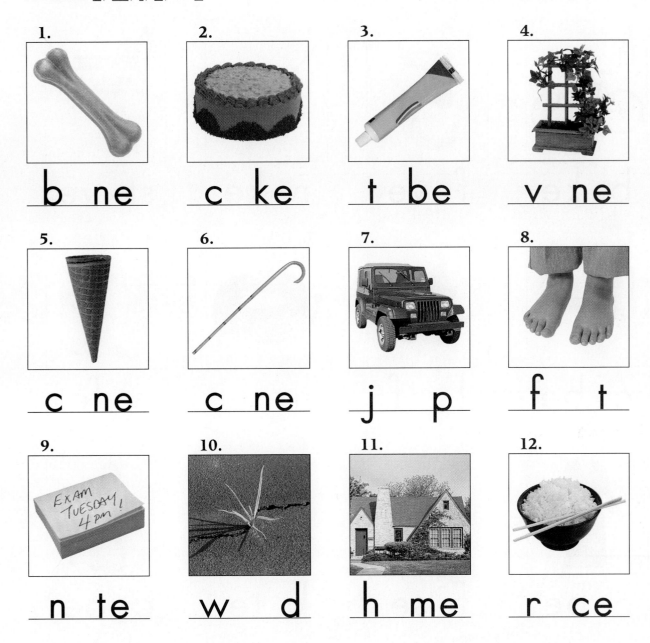

1. b __ ne

2. c __ ke

3. t __ be

4. v __ ne

5. c __ ne

6. c __ ne

7. j __ p

8. f __ t

9. n __ te

10. w __ d

11. h __ me

12. r __ ce

Instructor's Notes: Read the directions. Review all picture names: 1 bone, 2 cake, 3 tube, 4 vine, 5 cone, 6 cane, 7 jeep, 8 feet, 9 note, 10 weed, 11 home, 12 rice. Have students write the missing letter to finish each word.

B. Write a, ea, i, o, or u.

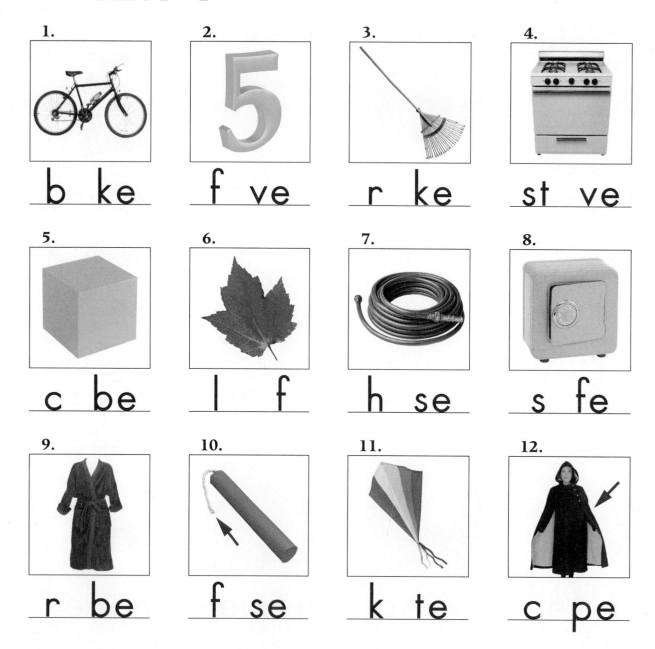

1. b___ke

2. f___ve

3. r___ke

4. st___ve

5. c___be

6. l___f

7. h___se

8. s___fe

9. r___be

10. f___se

11. k___te

12. c___pe

Instructor's Notes: Read the directions. Review all picture names: 1 bike, 2 five, 3 rake, 4 stove, 5 cube, 6 leaf, 7 hose, 8 safe, 9 robe, 10 fuse, 11 kite, 12 cape. Have students write the missing letter to finish each word.

A. Write the letter.

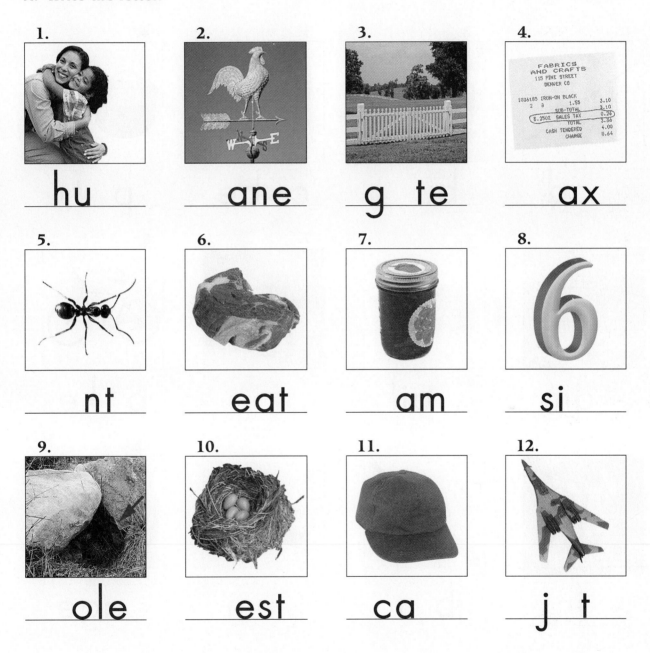

1. hu ____

2. ____ ane

3. g ____ te

4. ____ ax

5. ____ nt

6. ____ eat

7. ____ am

8. si ____

9. ____ ole

10. ____ est

11. ca ____

12. j ____ t

Instructor's Notes: Read the directions. Review all picture names: 1 hug, 2 vane, 3 gate, 4 tax, 5 ant, 6 meat, 7 jam, 8 six, 9 hole, 10 nest, 11 cap, 12 jet. Have students write the missing letter to finish each word.

B. Write the letter.

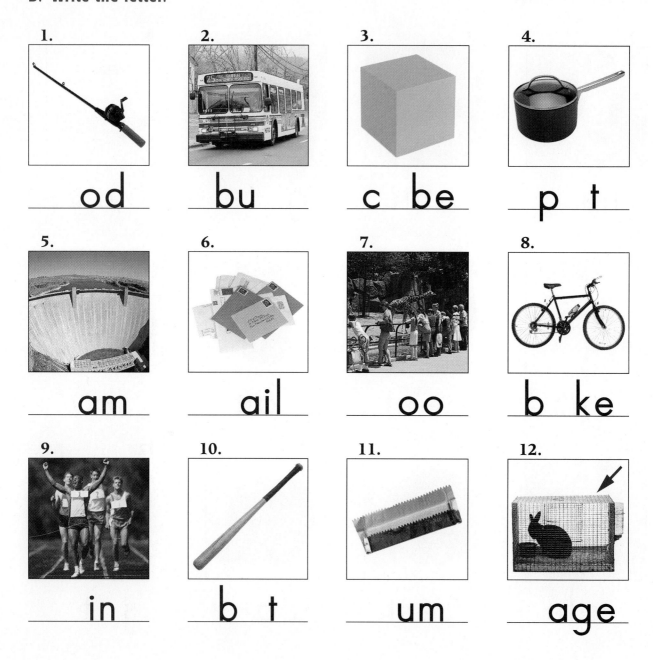

1. __ od

2. bu __

3. c __ be

4. p __ t

5. __ am

6. __ ail

7. __ oo

8. b __ ke

9. __ in

10. b __ t

11. __ um

12. __ age

Instructor's Notes: Read the directions. Review all picture names: 1 rod, 2 bus, 3 cube, 4 pot, 5 dam, 6 mail, 7 zoo, 8 bike, 9 win, 10 bat, 11 gum, 12 cage. Have students write the missing letter to finish each word.

C. Write the letter or letters.

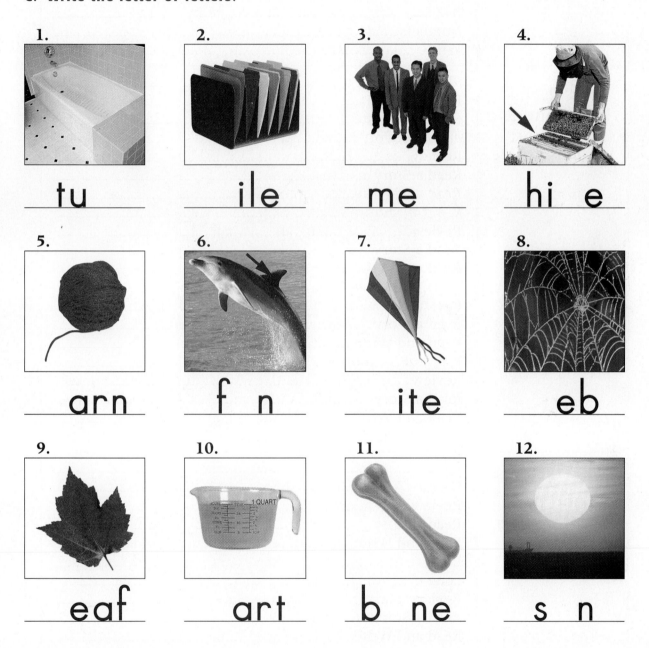

1. tu____

2. ____ile

3. me____

4. hi__e

5. ____arn

6. f__n

7. ____ite

8. ____eb

9. ____eaf

10. ____art

11. b__ne

12. s__n

Instructor's Notes: Read the directions. Review all picture names: 1 tub, 2 file, 3 men, 4 hive, 5 yarn, 6 fin, 7 kite, 8 web, 9 leaf, 10 quart, 11 bone, 12 sun. Have students write the missing letter or letters to finish each word. Use Blackline Master 8: Certificate of Completion from the *Reading for Today Instructor's Guide* when the student successfully completes this book.

Unit	Skill	Completion	Date
1 Letters of the Alphabet	Aa–Ff	☐	_____
	Gg–Ll	☐	_____
	Mm–Rr	☐	_____
	Ss–Zz	☐	_____
	A–Z	☐	_____
	Numbers	☐	_____
	Write	☐	_____
2 Consonant and Short Vowel Sounds	m, d, f, g, short a	☐	_____
	Review	☐	_____
	Read and Write	☐	_____
	b, t, s, w, short o	☐	_____
	Review	☐	_____
	Read a Story	☐	_____
	Read and Write	☐	_____
	k, j, p, n, short i	☐	_____
	Review	☐	_____
	Read a Story	☐	_____
	Read and Write	☐	_____
	c, h, l, r, short u	☐	_____
	Review	☐	_____
	Read a Story	☐	_____
	Read and Write	☐	_____
	v, y, z, qu, x, short e	☐	_____
	Review	☐	_____
	Read a Story	☐	_____
	Read and Write	☐	_____
	Unit 2 Review	☐	_____
3 Long and Short Vowels	Long a	☐	_____
	Long i	☐	_____
	Review	☐	_____
	Read a Story	☐	_____
	Read and Write	☐	_____
	Long o	☐	_____
	Long u	☐	_____
	Review	☐	_____
	Read a Story	☐	_____
	Read and Write	☐	_____
	Long e	☐	_____
	Review	☐	_____
	Read a Story	☐	_____
	Read and Write	☐	_____
	Read a Story	☐	_____
	Think About It	☐	_____
	Unit 3 Review	☐	_____
	Final Review	☐	_____